EAST CENTRAL AFRICA

EAST CENTRAL AFRICA
KENYA, UGANDA, TANZANIA, RWANDA, AND BURUNDI

BY F. BLANCHE FOSTER

FRANKLIN WATTS
New York | London | Toronto | Sydney | 1981
A FIRST BOOK

A GROLIER COMPANY

Cover design by Jackie Schuman

Photographs courtesy of:
Embassy of the Republic of Uganda: pp. 3, 23, 53;
Photo Researchers, Inc./Jen and Des Bartlett: p. 8;
Rapho/Photo Researchers, Inc./Ray Ellis: p. 13;
World Bank Photo by Yutaka Nagata: p. 17;
WHO Photo by R. Seitz: p. 18;
Sygma/William Campbell: p. 30;
Rapho/Photo Researchers, Inc./Lynn Millar: p. 35;
Rapho/Photo Researchers, Inc./Lynn McLaven: p. 39;
WHO Photo by D. Henrioud: p. 41;
Diane Rawson/Photo Researchers, Inc.: p. 46;
United Press International: p. 50.

Maps courtesy of Vantage Art

Library of Congress Cataloging in Publication Data

Foster, F   Blanche.
East Central Africa.

(A First book)
Bibliography: p.
Includes index.
SUMMARY: Discusses the geography, industry, and way
of life of five countries of East Central Africa.
1. Africa, East—Juvenile literature.   2. Rwanda—
Juvenile literature.   3. Burundi—Juvenile literature.
[1. Africa, East.   2. Rwanda.   3. Burundi]   I. Title.
DT423.F67   1981   967   80-26847
ISBN 0-531-04272-3

CONTENTS

To Betty, Dianne,
and Paula Crain

WESTERN
SAHARA

CAPE
VERDE

SENEGAL

GAMBIA

GUINEA
BISSAU

SIERRA LEONE

LIBERIA

MAURITANIA

MALI

UPPER
VOLTA

GUINEA

IVORY
COAST

GHANA

TOGO

BENIN

NIGER

NIGERIA

CHAD

SUDAN

DJIBOUTI

CAMEROON

CENTRAL
AFRICAN REPUBLIC

ETHIOPIA

EQUATORIAL GUINEA

SAO TOME & PRINCIPE

GABON

CONGO

ZAIRE

UGANDA

KENYA

SOMALIA

RWANDA
BURUNDI

TANZANIA

SEYCHELLE

ANGOLA

ZAMBIA

MALAWI

MOZAMBIQUE

COMORO
ISLANDS

MADAGASCAR

MAURITIU

NAMIBIA

ZIMBABWE

REUNIO

BOTSWANA

SWAZILAND

LESOTHO

Africa

SOUTH
AFRICA

1
EAST CENTRAL
AFRICA

The region of East Central Africa is made up of five countries: Burundi, Rwanda, Kenya, Tanzania, and Uganda. Although the countries share a geographical location, they have their own separate identities. Yet they all share such natural attractions as lakes, rivers, valleys, wildlife, and cool weather. In these countries live some of the shortest and the tallest people in the world.

An outstanding geographical feature that four of the countries share is the Great Rift Valley. It runs through Burundi, Rwanda, Kenya, and Tanzania. It is believed that the Rift Valley was caused by movements on the continent of Africa millions of years ago when a block of land sank into the crusts of the earth. This created a northbound valley with steep walls as high as a mile. The Rift Valley is 20 to 30 miles (32 to 48 km) wide and runs over 3,000 miles (4,800 km) from south to north. There are numerous rivers and lakes in the region, and the climate is temperate and mild.

Wildlife abounds in this region. Seen throughout the area are antelope, boars, cheetahs, civet, cobs, duikers, elephants, flying lemurs, gazelles, impalas, jackals, leopards, and giraffes. Gorillas, hartebeests, hippopotamuses, hyenas, and lions live in the area. Mangabeys, reedbuck, rhinoceroses, topi warthogs, waterbuck, wildebeests, and zebras are among the reasons tourists visit East Central Africa.

Game birds and other birds add to the fascination of the land. Some of them have strange names such as bulbul, hoopoe, ibis, kite, lourie, weaver, shrike, and snipe. Birds with descriptive names like crowned crane, lily-trotter, bee-eater, and the mousebird may be seen. In the area are also the egret, guinea, fowl, heron, and the partridge. The peaceful dove lives quietly with the eagle, quail, stork, and the exotic flamingo.

Some of the trees have strange or descriptive names. There are the podo and baobab trees with oil palm, pencil cedar, and the African camphor. Familiar trees include coconut, fig, olive, acacia, and eucalyptus.

The people of East Central Africa share lakes, rivers, mountains, an ocean, and the Equator. Lake Victoria, the second largest freshwater lake in the world, is shared by Kenya, Tanzania, and Uganda. Known as Victoria Nyanza to the people living in the area, this lake has an area of 26,828 square miles (69,485 sq km). It is the source of the Nile River which runs through Uganda. Rwanda, Tanzania, and Uganda share the Kagera River which flows into Lake Victoria.

Lake Tanganyika, the second deepest lake in the world, lies on the border of Tanzania and Burundi. It is over 3,700 feet (1,128 m) deep, has an elevation of 2,534 feet (772 m) above sea level and is 12,700 square miles (32,893 sq km) in area. History records the eastern shore of Lake Tanganyika as the place where Henry Stanley, a British newspaper reporter, found Dr. Livingston, a missionary long thought lost, in 1871.

The highest elevation in Africa is Mount Kilimanjaro. It graces Tanzania and Kenya's border and rises to 19,340 feet

Elephants are only one of the many types of wild and exotic animals that make their home in East Central Africa.

(5,895 m) above sea level. Coffee flourishes on the lower slopes of this extinct volcano. The mountain has two peaks. Kibo, the highest, is always ringed with white clouds and covered with snow. Kenya and Tanzania also share the Indian Ocean on their eastern borders.

Since all five countries lie on or near the Equator, one would think that the area would be very hot. The opposite is true, however, since the mountains and plateaus keep many areas pleasant and cool. In areas where it is warmer, there may be grasslands (savannas) on wetlands near forests. Some grass can grow 11 or 12 feet (over 3 m) high. Snakes such as the cobra and mamba often live there.

While the people of these countries share many of the geo-graphical features of this region, they have many differences as well. Historical differences among ethnic groups have persisted and often create discord among the people.

2
KENYA

Kenya is endowed with an unusual physical beauty, fine natural resources, and a history of a desire to be free. Covering an area of 224,960 square miles (582,646 sq km) including 5,300 square miles (13,727 sq km) of water, it is bounded by the Indian Ocean on the southeast and Lake Victoria on the southwest. Tanzania borders the south; on the northwest corner is the Sudan; and on the eastern border is Somalia. Though the country is situated on the equator, its mountains and highlands keep the fertile farmlands cool.

In 700 A.D., Muslims from South Arabia came to the coast of Kenya where they colonized the area, setting up trade and cities. Seven hundred years later, Portuguese were defeated by Arabs and forced to leave on their arrival in the area in 1498. The coming of the Europeans marked the beginning of one of the greatest struggles for freedom on the continent of Africa.

Captain Frederick Lugard of Great Britain arrived in Kenya with an expedition in 1890. Lured by the pleasant climate and fertile land, he set up the British East Africa Company, an organization which gave away important Kenyan land for British profit.

Lugard's expedition wreaked havoc in Kenya. The white man was determined to make Kenya "White Man's Land." The Kenyans were resettled; thousands were killed, and hundreds of thousands of sheep, goats, and cattle were stolen by the British. In less than six years, over a million acres of land had been taken by the British through treaties and theft. Ten years later, over a thousand farmers from Europe laid claim to more than 5 million acres (2,025,000 hectares) of the finest land in Kenya which they called "The White Highlands." The stage was set for the Kenyans to revolt and reclaim what was theirs. It took them more than fifty years to make Kenya again "The Black Man's Land."

JOMO KENYATTA

Harry Thuku was the first nationalist leader of Kenya. He organized Kenyans of all backgrounds to rebel against the British laws in 1921. The following year he was arrested. As a crowd of followers attempted to rescue him, twenty-one people were killed and hundreds seriously wounded. Thuku was deported and detained for eight years. Jomo Kenyatta, one of his followers, took up the battle for Kenya and its struggle for freedom.

Jomo Kenyatta was born in 1895 near Nairobi. As a child, he saw the barbed wire fences and soldiers with guns determined to keep his people in a restricted area. After attending a mission-

The second highest mountain in Africa, Mount Kenya, rises to a height of 17,040 feet (5,180 m).

ary school, he was given the Christian name of Johnstone and had the training as a minor civil servant of the colonial government.

Kenyatta used his education well. He was a court interpreter and became supervisor in the Nairobi water department. His studies abroad widened his influence, bringing him into contact with communists, socialists, and liberals; with Americans and people from the West Indies. His visits took him to Germany and Russia. Having excelled at the London School of Economics, he became well prepared to become president of the Kenya African Union and took the responsibilities of that office in 1947. Shortly afterward he was arrested as the leader of the "Mau Mau."

"Mau Mau" was a term coined by the British for an organization headed by Kenyatta, properly known as the Freedom Struggle Association. The Kikuyu, Kenya's largest ethnic group, played the leading role in the freedom association. By 1952, hundreds of thousands had taken the oath of unity to free Kenya from its oppression and to return Kenyans' land stolen or ceded to Britain.

During the 1940s and '50s, little progress had been made toward interracial cooperation. In 1944 an African was appointed to the Legislative Council. The first African was appointed to the Council of Ministers in 1954. These acts did not allow Kenyans a voice of confidence in terms of African leadership. Naturally, resentment resulted, and political confusion followed.

The new multiracial government satisfied neither the Kenyans nor the British. The first real African elections were held in 1961. The two political parties (KANU and KADU) campaigned for Jomo Kenyatta's release from prison. He was released, came home on August 14, 1961, and took office as Kenya's first Prime Minister in June 1963. Freedom (*uhuru*) came to Kenya as Mzee Jomo Kenyatta became President of the Republic of Kenya on December 12, 1964, within the British Commonwealth.

WORKING TOGETHER

President Kenyatta was faced with many problems stemming from friction among the different ethnic groups in the country. He urged his country to lay aside "tribalism" and to adhere to the principle of *harambee* (pulling together). He organized his cabinet so that the young and old were equally represented. Everything went rather smoothly until the assassination of Tom Mboya, a Luo and the minister of economic planning. The old wounds of "tribalism" were reopened. After Kenyatta again urged all Kenyans to participate in the government policy-making and lowering the voting age to eighteen, *harambee* appeared to take the upper hand.

President Kenyatta became a symbol of peace and progress to his Kenyan citizens as he remained at the head of his beloved country until his death on August 22, 1978. Vice-President Daniel arap Moi became interim President and was elected by a large voting turnout on November 8, 1979, to head the country. This election signaled the importance of "pulling together" regardless of ethnic origin as Philip Leakey also became the first white member of Parliament since Kenya's independence. An Indian lawyer, Khrishna Gautama, won a cabinet seat as Kenya's first Asian member of Parliament.

Kenya's population is an international one. There are nearly fifteen million Kenyans including the non-African minorities of 139,000 Asians, 40,000 Europeans, and 28,000 Arabs. The ethnic groups among the African population include the Kikuyu, Kamba, Luo, Luyia, Turkana, Pokot, Kipsigis, and Tugen. The Masai receive much publicity and attention throughout the world because they have resisted the political, social, and educational changes of Kenya. Retaining their age-old custom of a nomadic life-style and raising cattle, the Masai seem convinced that their pastoral way of life is superior.

The larger cities and towns contain most of Kenya's population. Nairobi, which means "the place of cool water," is the capital and has a population of more than 600,000. Pleasantly cooled by its height above sea level, it is considered one of the most scenic and architecturally beautiful capitals of the world. Mombasa, Kenya's oldest city, is one of the largest ports on the east coast of Africa. Today it combines the exotic past of Arabian Nights, Hawaiian serenity, Oriental aromas and colors, busy waterways, and African realism into one of the most exciting cities on the Indian Ocean. Other cities with large populations include Nakuru, Kisumu, and Eldoret.

Agriculture is the most important source of income for Kenya. The several cash crops produced include coffee, tea, maize, wheat, sugar, sisal, coconuts, barley, pineapples, and pyrethrum. Coffee is the principal export. Other exports are meat and meat products, hides and skins, manufactured goods like

A skyline view of Nairobi shows
the poverty and overcrowding that
exist on the outskirts of the city.

soda ash, cement, and petroleum products. The main imports are crude petroleum, motor vehicles, agricultural machinery and tractors, electrical and industrial machinery, iron and steel, fertilizers, and pharmaceutical products. Marked advancement is being made in the fields of mining, industry, manufacturing, and forestry. Fishing still has a prominent role.

Tourism is almost as important to Kenya's economy as its export of coffee. Just as Switzerland "sells" her lofty mountains and ski resorts and the West Indies their beaches, so does Kenya "sell" its landscaping, waters, mountains, and animals. People from all parts of the world come on safaris to visit Kenya's game parks, lakes, and cities.

The many national parks and game reserves of Kenya are located in a variety of climates and scenery. In any of these parks, one can see herds of elephants, buffalo, rhinoceroses, giraffes, lions, leopards and zebras. National parks are also located in the mountain ranges of Mt. Elgon, and on snowcapped Mt. Kenya. In Aberdares National Park there is a hotel built on stilts in the heart of the wild game land from which tourists can view herds of elephants, buffalo, and other animals walking together and frolicking at a nearby water hole.

EDUCATION
While Kenya was under British rule, education for Africans was maintained at a very low level. But as independence drew near,

Small birds hitch a ride
on the neck of a giraffe
in a Kenyan park.

many improvements were made in the system. The number of primary and secondary schools increased dramatically, and schools that were closed to Africans under British rule were integrated. There are many secondary schools, teacher training institutions, technical schools, and two universities. In addition, thousands of Kenyans leave the country to study in other parts of the world preparing to continue the concept of *harambee*.

KEEPING TRADITIONS ALIVE

The cultures and traditions of the people of Kenya are kept alive through their religious and fine arts. Fine arts are woven into their daily lives through festivals, educational programs, and story telling. Without imposing their traditions upon other groups in the country, each group seeks refinement, individuality, and high quality in their art, dance, and even religion.

All art forms are used to strengthen the cultures of Kenya. The Masai women use their beautiful beadwork to make collars and necklaces. Often they make special necklaces that are worn only at their weddings and festivals when the men combine their dancing and music to express their courage. The men also excel in making spears and shields.

The carvings and decorated calabashes of Kenya are displayed in homes and museums throughout the world. A calabash grows on a climbing vine, and resembles a squash or a pumpkin. It is a gourd and has a tough, hard outer shell and is often used

*A secondary school
in Nairobi, Kenya*

as a cooking pot in many parts of Africa. Calabashes can be carved and made into containers as well as musical instruments. The Kamba, living southeast of Nairobi in a harsh landscaped town called Ukamba, are given credit as some of the best carvers and decorators of calabashes.

An artist named Peter Nzuki is highly praised for his calabash decorations. Nzuki became a great artist through his interest in his own cultural heritage. Having learned about the art history of calabash carving, he decided to revive the art. Using his country's animals as subjects, Nzuki carves designs into the outer crust. He uses geometric designs and circular patterns to create representations of the cobra, python, other animals and people. The National Museum in Nairobi houses some of Nzuki's works.

A Kenyan woman completes
a wall sampler that she will
then sell to buy more and
better food for her family.

3

UGANDA

Many anthropologists believe that Uganda was the site of human beginnings in East Africa. There is also evidence that a part of the Stone Age industry existed there. Pygmies of western Uganda left evidence of their hunting tools. Other groups left proof of their hand ax industry. It is believed that agriculture and animal domestication first occurred there with other East African countries. Some historians surmise that iron was also developed in Uganda.

Uganda has been the site, through the years, of many migrations from nearby countries. It has been claimed that the first migrations into Uganda took place as early as the fourth century A.D. People came into Uganda from neighboring Sudan to the north, from Zaire to the west, Rwanda and Burundi to the southwest, and Tanzania to the south.

For centuries Uganda was the site of strong, traditional kingdoms which ruled the country. The Ankole, Buganda, and Bunyoro kingdoms held the power for many years, the Bunyoro-Kitara Kingdom holding the leadership position until the 1880s.

Many exotic and strange stories have been told and written about the governments and peoples of the kingdoms of Uganda. Arabs and visitors from foreign lands have described highly civilized and intelligent forms of government which existed in Uganda. Foreigners often said that the homes were so gracious, well-appointed, and clean that the Ugandan's way of life was superior to their own.

There are many different ethnic groups in Uganda, separated most often by differences in language. Bantu languages are spoken by most of the people in southern Uganda. Nilotic and Luo languages were spoken in the Buganda and Bunyoro areas along with the influence of Bantu speaking groups. The largest ethnic group in Uganda is the Baganda who live on the northern shore of Lake Victoria. Other groups include the Banyoro, Banyankole, Batoro, Iteso, Lango, Achole, and Karamojong. In an effort to settle the language problem, Swahili is to become the official language for all citizens, although English has been spoken since independence.

The ability of the different kingdoms to get along well enough to form a workable form of government was a quality greatly admired by visitors. During the middle of the eighteenth century when Arabs and Europeans made trips to Eastern Africa, many Ugandans were converted to Christianity and Islam. It was during this time that the large and powerful kingdom of Bunyoro-Kitara was challenged for supremacy by Buganda. The king of Buganda, Mutesa I, welcomed the British and missionaries to his kingdom in the hope that he could use them for his own purposes.

Mutesa was not as interested in Christianity as he was in seeking assistance from the Europeans against the threatening Egyptians nearby. After the missionaries showed no interest in the military affairs of Buganda, Mutesa became less friendly

*A hungry crocodile in the Murchison Falls National Park
in Uganda shows its rows of large, uneven teeth.*

toward them. He died in 1884, after which his son Mwanga became king of Buganda.

Mwanga was very hostile toward both the Christians and Arabs because he felt they had too much influence over his people. During his reign, confrontations between him and his people arose because of his attitude. The Arabs, missionaries, and Bugandan converts joined forces to drive Mwanga from the country. Persecution and hostility erupted in great force while the two factions fought.

GREAT BRITAIN GAINS CONTROL

During the great land-grabbing rush of the mid-nineteenth century, Uganda was a place Europeans wanted very eagerly to control. The British population in the country had grown to the extent that the Imperial British East African Company was granted a charter to control the British interest there. Great Britain continued power in Uganda through fighting and winning small battles over some of the smaller kingdoms. By 1896 Great Britain was in control of most of what is known today as Uganda. The following year Mwanga waged war against Great Britain, but was defeated and deposed. His son, Daudi Chwa, became the next king, although he was at the time only an infant.

Criticisms were leveled at Great Britain for its military campaigns and the amount of money spent on them. Britain attempted to offset this by establishing a civil administration throughout Uganda. In 1900 the chiefs of Buganda signed an agreement which gave Great Britain indirect control of Buganda. Later the remaining kingdoms signed treaties.

The agreement changed the way of life for Ugandans. It decreed that the kings could keep their kingdoms and have power to select their own men to sit in Parliament (Lukiko). Great Britain took land which was called "Crown" land from the King for use by Britons only. A portion of the land was then given back to the people on the condition they pay taxes to the British!

The British Commissioner gave power to the Lukiko to make laws which they thought best for Uganda. They decided that the Buganda government would rule over Buganda and that the central government would rule over all of Uganda. Consequently, Buganda became the favored kingdom, the British granting it greater advantages. Daudi Chwa ruled Buganda until his death in 1939 and was succeeded by his son, Kabaka Mutesa II, who ruled until independence.

World War I had minimum effects upon the citizens of Uganda. The country was too concerned with its own problems. The introduction of goods for export changed the lives of many Ugandans. Prior to 1900 the only export was ivory. After the emphasis upon growing cotton, sugar, and coffee, many Ugandans became farmers. Indians were brought to the country by the British to help build railroads and work in industry in the growing and processing of these products.

After the end of World War II, many political riots took place since the Ugandans were stirred by the meaning of "freedom."

THE FIGHT FOR INDEPENDENCE

With the end of World War II, many African nations—including Uganda—started movements to gain independence from the European nations that had exploited them for so long.

Political riots at first centered around problems within the country. The internal problems of Buganda were at stake. To ease the situation, the British exiled Mutesa II since they felt that he was the cause of the problem. The Bugandans considered this an offense, and it only created tension between the British and Buganda.

Buganda decided that it could settle the issue by separating from Uganda and becoming an independent country. The British refused to accept this demand. As the commercial center and wealthiest province of Uganda, Buganda would greatly damage the rest of the country by separating from it. It was agreed later that the Lukiko would be given even greater power. The members of Parliament would elect whomever they wanted as king; set up government departments; and work toward self-governing of their own state under the majority of Ugandans. National elections were to be held in 1958.

In an effort to keep Uganda unified before the elections, the king of Buganda was offered the position of king of Uganda with a federal state of Buganda as the leading state. This created greater opposition to Buganda from other Ugandans. When elections were held, Buganda refused to vote. Over 80 percent of Ugandans voted, giving Uganda an opportunity to fight for one nation. Even with all this conflict, Uganda reached independence in October 1962. The way was paved for election of governmental officials.

Dr. Milton Obote was elected Prime Minister. King Mutesa II, who had returned from exile in London earlier, was elected President of the Republic of Uganda.

Uganda had been divided into four regions for many years. Each region contained four to seven districts. The regions were

Buganda, Eastern, Northern, and Western. In a sense, each region was a kingdom. After independence, friction between these regions caused great strain to Uganda.

Buganda's position as the leader of the country was resented by the other regions. Obote's party had obtained a majority of members in Parliament. After many disagreements, Obote suspended the constitution and gave himself full executive powers. In April 1966 he presented a new constitution with himself as President.

As President, Obote removed the federal status of Buganda and abolished the other kingdoms. Since Kampala, the capital of Uganda, is located in Buganda, the Lukiko asked the central government to leave their soil. The regular army stormed the palace of the Kabaka three days later. Mutesa II escaped and fled to London.

It was a costly way to unify Uganda. Buganda was divided into four districts. The army became the target of resentment because of the number of lives lost in the change of government. Obote tried to find a solution for support of a feeling of nationalism among all Ugandans.

He introduced his "Common Man's Charter" which he hoped would equalize all regions. In spite of his efforts, he was resented by some and was wounded in an assassination attempt in 1969. Nevertheless, he continued to work toward economic and commercial improvement. He set the next election for April 1971. After the announcement, he left the country for a meeting in Singapore. While he was away, Major-General Idi Amin took power over Uganda on January 25, 1971. He later proclaimed himself President for Life.

IDI AMIN

The military regime of President for Life Idi Amin lasted eight years. During that time he was labeled a dictator and a murderer. A month after he became President he changed the constitution to abolish rights regarding freedom from certain arrests, expression, assembly, and movement. This gave the Armed Forces almost complete power to search and seize property and limit the freedom of the people.

During his eight years in office he forced all Asians (many of whom dominated the commerce and industry of the country) to flee. He also killed hundreds of thousands of Ugandans, from all regions of the country. The British were also expelled from the country. There was an attempt to assassinate Amin, but it failed. Several countries throughout the world imposed trade sanctions against Uganda, damaging its already sagging economy.

Finally, in March 1979, rebels from Uganda and soldiers from Tanzania invaded the capital city, Kampala. They were victorious over Amin's army and forced him to fly to Libya with his family where he remained until May 1980. It has been reported that he later left, making his new home in Saudi Arabia.

Electing a president for Uganda has been difficult. Yusifi K. Lule became the leader after Amin but lasted only two months. He was followed by Godfrey Binaisa. In May 1980 the military commission ousted Binaisa. In thirteen months changes had been swift in the turnover of power. There are many supporters of Dr. Obote, who now lives in Tanzania. It is believed that thousands of Ugandans would be very happy if he would return as president of Uganda.

Once considered the leading country in East Africa, Uganda is most scenic and blessed with many natural resources. Its capital, Kampala, meaning "hill of the antelope," is situated on seven hills. Enhancing the surroundings of the hills are palaces and imposing government buildings. There are beautiful gardens and sloping lawns to add to the scenery. Other large cities include Jinja and Njeru, Mbale, Entebbe, and Gulu.

Before 1971 Ugandans had several ways to make a living. They were involved in agriculture, mining, fishing, and industry. Production of cotton, copper, and sugar added to Uganda's foreign trade. But once Amin took over, Uganda reverted to a subsistence economy. During his reign nearly 90 percent of the population depended exclusively on what they themselves were able to grow. Industrial development ceased completely, and the total breakdown of the road and rail system added to the economy's rapid decline.

THE STRUGGLE FOR HUMAN VALUES

Kampala is a city surrounded by beautiful gardens, sloping lawns, and palaces. But this scenic beauty exists in sharp contrast to the misery and poverty endured by many Ugandans today. The effects of Idi Amin's regime, the subsequent quest for individual power, and squabbles among different ethnic groups have led to persecutions, famine, and starvation for a large segment of the population.

The Karamojong district of northern Uganda has received worldwide attention for the suffering there. It is claimed that starvation there parallels or surpasses that of the Sahel, the Horn of Africa, parts of Zimbabwe, and Mozambique. The media has shown countless numbers of children and adults wandering in hordes awaiting a food plane or truck. Others simply await death.

[29]

It is somewhat ironic that a country which had done so much to combat malaria, sleeping-sickness, and leprosy among its people would now suffer the effects of starvation. Many Ugandan children have *kwashiorkor*.

Kwashiorkor is a serious disease that affects mainly children who do not receive the essential minerals, vitamins, and protein from their diet. Protein is necessary for the repair and growth of body tissues. Where there is little or no food as in Karamojong district, it is no surprise that *kwashiorkor* afflicts most of the young children there. *Kwashiorkor* is recognized by bloated bellies, black hair turning red, and stunted physical growth. Mental impairment usually occurs with this disease.

While many parts of the world are concerned about the condition of the Karamojong, the Acholi and others in Uganda create songs, dances, and stories to tell of the plight of the starving ones.

A Karamojong villager and his herd of cattle reflect the recent starvation and suffering in the area.

TANZANIA

Tanzania, the largest country in East Africa, lies just south of the Equator. Its mainland is between the area of the great lakes Victoria, Tanganyika, and Malawi. The Indian Ocean borders the east. The total area is 362,688 square miles (939,361 sq km) which includes 19,982 square miles (51,752 sq km) of inland water. Uganda and Kenya bound Tanzania on the north, Mozambique and Malawi on the south, Zambia on the southwest with Zaire, Burundi, and Rwanda on the west.

Tanzania's mountains and lakes are famous for their beauty and historical significance. Africa's highest mountain, Kilimanjaro, adds to the beauty of Tanzania in the north. Mt. Usambara lies in the northeast with Livingstone and Ufipa Highlands in the south and southwest. Lake Tanganyika, the world's longest freshwater lake and one of the deepest, makes up part of the inland water on the western border. Lake Victoria graces Tanzania's north. Other lakes include Malawi, Natron, Eyasi, Rukwa, and Manyara.

HISTORY
The history of Tanzania is a colorful one. Arabs lived with Africans there from the eighth through the sixteenth centuries as

they intermarried and created the Swahili language. Religious persecutions in Arabia brought many Persians and Arabs to the coastal region of Africa. The ugly part of this history concerns one of the world's largest slave markets.

It was controlled by Arabs. They took the slaves in boats to Arabia and India if they were not needed in Zanzibar—an island off the coast of Tanzania—where the market was located. There the slaves were used mainly to carry ivory which was then sold for great profit. As many as seven thousand slaves were sold each year. Several revolts occurred between Africans and Arabs, but it was not until the British stepped in that the problem was finally solved. The Sultans who controlled Zanzibar finally signed a treaty with the British to stop the slave trade. The market was closed in 1873.

The first Europeans to come to Tanzania were the Portuguese. They tried to settle in Zanzibar but were defeated in 1699 by Arabs from Oman. Later explorers from Great Britain were upset by the slave trade, and, when they reported what they had seen, missionaries were sent to Tanzania. With these Europeans also came the scramble for control over East Africa, and ownership of its resources.

In 1885, Karl Peters from Germany secured a grant for an imperial charter giving Germany an East Africa Company. The

The Arab influence is evident in the architecture as well as the dress of the local merchants in this street in Zanzibar.

Anglo-German Agreement of 1886 stated that their control should be divided by a line running from south of Mombasa (Kenya), north of Kilimanjaro to a point on the eastern shore of Lake Victoria. The British were given Zanzibar.

Tanzania remained under the German government for twenty years. During that time, the Germans concentrated on improving methods of farming and building railroads. When World War I came, and Germany lost the war to the Allies, the British took over the land and renamed it Tanganyika. This name remained after the independence of Tanzania.

Another result of the war was that the British returned some power to the African chiefs whose authority had been lessened by the Germans. With an alliance between the British and Africans, an effort was made to rebuild the economy. Success was being made until World War II erupted, when Tanganyika became a trustee of the United Nations under British protection. As the fervor for freedom and independence spread throughout Africa, Tanzania prepared for its great day. On December 9, 1961, Tanzania emerged from British colonialism and became an independent member of the British Commonwealth. One day later, Julius K. Nyerere was elected President.

President Nyerere was born in 1922 and spent his childhood herding cattle for his father. After being educated in missionary schools, he left for Great Britain where he received advanced training as a teacher. He returned to his homeland in 1952 as one of the few university graduates in Tanzania. He was interested in the welfare of all his country's people, and his work with the constitution of Tanzania's only political party showed his concern for their progress.

The Tanganyika African National Union (TANU) formed

its objectives early based upon the principles of Dr. Nyerere. The objectives stressed the following goals:

> *Preparation of the people for self-government and independence, and to fight relentlessly until Tanganyika is self-governing and independent.*
>
> *To fight against tribalism and other tendencies among Africans, and to build up a united nationalism.*
>
> *To fight relentlessly for the establishment of a democratic form of government, to fight for the introduction of the election principle in all bodies of local and central government.*
>
> *To fight for the removal of every form of racialism and racial discrimination.*

Tanzanians admired and respected the dignity and intelligence of President Nyerere. They worked hard to make the constitution a reality. In the meantime, the island of Zanzibar had obtained independence in 1963, and on April 26, 1964, Zanzibar and Tanganyika signed an act of union and became one nation, Tanzania.

Dr. Nyerere continues to be returned to office during each election.

LIFE IN TANZANIA TODAY

Self-reliance for all of Tanzania has been the main goal of President Nyerere. On February 5, 1967, he announced the Arusha Declaration based on socialism and familyhood. With this plan all citizens, peasants and leaders alike, would work together

in dealing with the nation's domestic problems. The wealth would be equally distributed as every Tanzanian worked for self-reliance and the country's growth. The plan has been applauded by many observers as an excellent effort and model for countries seeking economic growth. Over five million people live in model villages as they cooperate to work toward Tanzania's future.

The population of Tanzania's mainland is estimated at about sixteen million. While some areas suffer from the tsetse fly and a lack of water, other areas are quite densely populated. The capital Dar es Salaam, meaning "haven of peace," is the largest city. Other cities include Tabora, Morogoro, Tanga, Mwanza, Arusha, Moshi, and Dodoma. President Nyerere hopes to move the capital from Dar es Salaam to Dodoma by 1985. The islands of Zanzibar and Pemba, which lie about 25 miles (39 km) off the coast, are densely populated and retain an urban atmosphere. Many smaller islands dot the Indian Ocean and are also a part of Tanzania.

There are many ethnic groups in Tanzania, 95 percent of whom are Bantu-speaking people. The largest group is the Sukuma, followed by the Nyamwezi, Ha, Makonde, Gogo, Chaga, and Hehe. Asians, Arabs, Europeans, Syrians, and some Chinese also live in Tanzania. Due to the early arrival of Arabs to the region, Islam is the predominant religion. There are also mil-

In Dar es Salaam, a child uses pieces of wood strung together to learn to count.

lions of Christians resulting from the work of European missionaries.

As in most other East Central African countries, agriculture is the mainstay of Tanzania's economy. Exports include sisal (a fiber used to make rope), diamonds, coffee, tea, tobacco, cloves, and petroleum. Many of Tanzania's imports—such as crude oil, cement, bicycles, and paint—come from other East African countries. Industry has been growing in recent years, with emphasis on fertilizer, paper, and wood production.

Education has top priority in the country. Before Mr. Nyerere's appearance as head of the government, the schools were segregated according to African, Asian, and European groups. This plan was abolished, and now that the schools are financed by the government, there is a single integrated system. The expansion of secondary education is highly encouraged. During 1980 there were over 9,000 primary schools, 35,000 secondary schools, and 2,050 schools of higher education. Children are required to attend school for seven years of primary education. The University College at Dar es Salaam trains students in law, art, science, medicine and other fields.

Tanzania's wildlife and varied countryside attract thousands of people from all parts of the world. Fascinating attractions are the game parks, beaches, cities, and Mount Kilimanjaro, the highest point in all Africa. The huge game parks and reserves of Serengeti, and Manyara have thousands of visitors each year to see the gazelles, zebras, and buffalo that migrate across the plains.

While living conditions are poor for many of the people of Tanzania, progress has been made in recent years. Health care

*A doctor interviews a woman and her child
at a district hospital in Tanzania.*

is still inadequate, and the infant mortality rate, while falling, is still quite high. The average life expectancy is still very low when compared to Western standards. Farming techniques are still primitive, and many areas continue to be plagued by the disease-carrying tsetse fly. Yet, the government has put a great deal of emphasis on education as well as on new industrial development.

THE ARTS

Dancing is a favorite entertainment for the people after a full day's work. Dancing to the pulsating rhythm of drums is an excellent form of exercise, a way to relieve tension, as well as a method of recreating some of the ritualistic past. This allows an opportunity to keep the traditional values and culture ever present among the people.

Storytelling is another form of entertainment. Keeping the audience entranced, the storyteller weaves a mystical aura while recreating past exploits, history, and satire. It has been stated that Tanzanians have refined the art of storytelling.

Collectors of African masks and ebony carvings have claimed that the work of the Makonde is among the finest. The Makonde are Tanzanians who live in the coastal regions and on the borders of Mozambique. In the past, most of the masks were considered sacred, to be used only in religious dances and rituals. The superiority of the Makonde carvings has been attributed to the classical traditions worked into their designs. The Makonde Helmet Mask, housed in the London Museum of Mankind, has been acclaimed as one of the finest traditional works of Africa. It is a sinuous figure carved in ebony depicting an Arab trader. Although it is carved in the traditional style, it uses human hair to present a realistic effect.

The Chagga people who live on the slopes of Mt. Kilimanjaro are craftsmen who work in wood. Using the abundant timber from the massive mountain, they make household utensils out of wood. Traditional values and culture are symbolized through their designs.

5
RWANDA AND BURUNDI

For many years historians have speculated, or guessed, about the beginnings of the two smallest countries in the East Africa community. All admit that they do not actually know how or when the first people came into the countries known today as Rwanda and Burundi. Some claim that hundreds of years ago pygmies known as the Twa lived in the land. Later they were joined by a taller group of people called the Hutu. The Hutu were known to be excellent farmers and good organizers.

A very tall group, probably from the north by way of the River Nile, came later. They were called the Tutsi. Historians say that the tall Tutsi overcame the shorter Hutu and made them serfs of the land. The Twa, living in forests and staying busy with their hunting and pottery, managed to separate themselves from the conflict.

In both Burundi and Rwanda, the Tutsi have always been outnumbered by the Hutu. In spite of this, the Tutsi managed to maintain control over the Hutu, a situation that bred resentment and anger between the people.

The twin kingdoms existed for hundreds of years. They were called Rwanda-Urundi. Each kingdom was ruled by a king called the *Mwami*. Because the two kingdoms did not share

each other's language and interests, they were not friendly and fought occasionally.

THE TWIN KINGDOMS

Since the fifteenth century, European traders had exploited Africa's rich resources and people. By the nineteenth century, the entire continent had been split up into colonial territories claimed for France, Spain, Portugal, and other European countries. In 1885 the major European powers met in Berlin and re-divided the continent.

The twin kingdoms of Rwanda-Urundi were given to Germany. The German government controlled the countries by allowing the Mwami in each kingdom to keep his power and rule the people. During the time between 1885–1914 Britain, France, and Germany began to rival each other for the allotted African territories. The twin kingdoms were involved in this rivalry and after World War I became a colony of Belgium.

As colonies of a foreign government, the countries found it gradually more difficult to tell foe from friend. Although the two were allowed to maintain their centuries old form of royalty, the Belgium government sought to merge Rwanda-Urundi with the Belgian Congo. The Europeans also encouraged the tall and proud Tutsi to control the kingdoms.

The Hutu showed their displeasure in being subjects of the minority Tutsi by staging a revolution in 1959. They killed many

A Tutsi mother and her children in Rwanda

Tutsi and others fled to neighboring countries. The Hutu were on their way to independence.

In 1961 the people of Rwanda-Urundi voted for separate governments. When the two countries (Urundi now called Burundi) became independent in 1962, Rwanda became a republic, but Burundi remained a monarchy. Mwami Ntare V remained in power until 1966 when Prime Minister Michael Micombero (a Tutsi) overthrew him and became Burundi's first President. The country was then declared a republic.

Meanwhile Rwanda had become a republic immediately upon separating from Burundi. President Gregoire Kayibanda remained in power until he was overthrown by an army coup in 1973.

The conflict between the physically taller Tutsi and the shorter Hutu continued throughout the 1970s. In 1972, the Hutu rebelled against their oppressors and killed about 1,000 Tutsi. The Tutsi retaliated by slaughtering an estimated 200,000 Hutu. This led to anger among the Hutu in Rwanda.

The Hutu there rounded up the Tutsi, killed them or forced them to flee to other countries. Tutsi students were even slaughtered. Finally, the military put an end to the killings and took over the government. General Juvenal Habarimana became President.

In 1976, Burundi's military overthrew President Micombero. General Jean-Baptist Bagaza was installed as their President. While there was no bloodshed in this takeover, the tension and upheavals have continued.

POVERTY AND OVERCROWDING

Burundi and Rwanda are two of the poorest and most overcrowded countries in Africa. There are 3,836,000 people in

Burundi living in an area of 10,747 square miles (27,835 sq km). Rwanda has 3,736,000 people living in 10,169 square miles (26,337 sq km). This is more than 350 people living in only one square mile (2.59 sq km).

Burundi is south of the Equator, bounded by Rwanda to the north and Tanzania to the east and south. Zaire, formerly known as the Congo, and Lake Tanganyika make up the western border. Rwanda is also bordered by Zaire on the west with Uganda on the north. Tanzania is the eastern border.

Bujumbura is the capital of Burundi with a population of 110,000. Kigali is Rwanda's capital and has a population of 59,000.

The climate of both countries is pleasant and cool since they are mountainous and have many plateaus. In Burundi it is a little warmer, especially around Lake Tanganyika. Rwanda has the Virunga Mountains which have a beautiful snowcapped peak. Mount Karisimbi, reaches 14,870 feet (4,532 m) above sea level.

Many rivers and lakes blend with the mountains and plateaus. The Akanyaru and Kageri Rivers flow through both countries. The Ruvubu and Malagarasi Rivers are at the southern part of Burundi. In Rwanda famous Lake Kivu is 4,700 feet (1,433 m) above sea level and drains into Lake Tanganyika through the Ruzizi River.

The social-political discord in Burundi and Rwanda had a bad effect upon the nations' economies. Already burdened by overpopulation, the countries have suffered. Both countries depend heavily upon agriculture as their main source of income. Coffee is the major cash crop. Other food crops include sweet potatoes, rice, maize, peas, beans, cassava, and sorghum.

The main exports from Burundi are coffee, cotton, hides

and skins, tea, and minerals. The imports are generally consumer goods such as food products. Rwanda imports cereals, petroleum products, cotton yarn and fabrics, and machinery. Their exports are coffee, which the United States purchases, tea, and tin ores. Presently, the governments are working to improve tobacco, forestry, and tea.

There is not much money among the people who live in these two very poor countries. About 90 percent of Rwanda's population live on small family farms and exist on the foods they are able to grow. The great majority of people in Burundi are also farmers and among the poorest people in Africa.

Activities in industry account for no more than 5 percent of the national budgets. In Burundi there are a few factories and plants for coffee processing, coffee ginning, the production of furniture, blankets, footwear, soap, and drinks. Rwanda fares a little better. There are some large-scale plants for processing coffee and tea, flour, cigars, beer, soft drinks, and assembling radios.

More than half the population of Burundi and Rwanda are Catholic, a result of the efforts of European missionaries. Over 80 percent of their schools are Catholic. After independence both countries gave the largest part of their budget for education. Great efforts have been made in recent years to educate the masses.

A typical scene at a market-
place in Bujumbura, Burundi,
one of the poorest and most
overcrowded countries in the world

Education is compulsory for all children to the age of fifteen in Rwanda. It is free to all children in Burundi between the ages of seven and fifteen. Students may continue their education through universities in both countries if they so wish. There are also four technical schools and a teacher training college. There is a university for Rwanda located at Butare, a city with a population of almost 600,000.

Religion is an important part of the life of most citizens of the twin kingdoms. Many worship the well-known religions of Catholicism, Protestantism, and Islam. The traditional religion of Imana has not lost its numerous followers, however.

Imana has as its main tenets the following concepts: a belief in God; obedience to God through word and action; and awareness that God sees all and knows all. Followers believe that God keeps in touch with them through their ancestors and through the spirits of the dead.

Burundi has been called a nation with a "rich African heritage, the customs of the people being unique and beautiful." Their dancing is classical with a great variety of musical instruments accompanying them. Their highly stylized rhythms are among the most intricate to be found in music. Tutsi dancing is graceful, with men moving in unison, their facial expressions

Though Rwanda and Burundi suffer from extreme poverty, money has been spent on national parks to help preserve the unusual animals, like the hippopotamus, that are native to the region.

portraying their refinement and confidence in themselves. The Hutu have added to the rich cultural heritage of the twin kingdoms through their world-famous folk songs.

There are museums, national parks and many scenic places for visitors. Lake Tanganyika in Burundi is visited by people from all over the world for its scenic beauty. In the southeast and northeast there are numerous animals and tropical birds. The former capital, Gitega, has a museum and a handicraft center.

Rwanda has the famous Lake Kivu, Kagera National Park, and the National Park of the Volcanoes. Scientists have made several trips to Lake Kivu, a lake in the Great Rift Valley. They believe there is a great supply of natural gas at the bottom of the lake which they think could be harnessed and used to meet the nation's energy needs. The national parks contain many rare forms of plant and animal life.

In these two nations, among the poorest in Africa, progress must be made in settling the differences between the Hutu and the Tutsi before the governments can concentrate on raising the standard of living for all the people.

FOR FURTHER READING

Encyclopedia of Africa, The. New York and London: Franklin Watts, 1977.

Hatch, John. *Tanzania: a Profile.* New York: Praeger, 1972.

Lemarchand, Rene. *Rwanda and Burundi.* London: Pall Mall, 1970.

Malatesta, Anne, and Friedland, Ronald. *The White Kikuyu, Louis B. Leakey.* New York: McGraw-Hill Book Company, 1978.

Martin, David. *General Amin.* London: Faber and Faber, 1974.

Murray-Brown, Jeremy. *Kenyatta.* New York: Dutton, 1973.

Nicholls, C. S. *The Swahili Coast.* London: Allen and Unwin, 1972.

Shorter, Aylward. *East African Societies.* London: Routledge & Kegan Paul, 1974.

INDEX

Crocodile, photo of, 23

Dar es Salaam, 38, 39
Dodoma, 39

Education
    Kenya, 15–17
    Rwanda-Burundi, 51–52
    Tanzania, 40–42
Eldoret, 12
Elephants, 2
Entebbe, 29
Equator, 2, 5, 7, 33, 49
Ethnic groups
    in Kenya, 10, 12
    in Tanzania, 39–40
    in Uganda, 22, 29
Europeans
    division of Africa, 47
    in Kenya, 7
    in Tanzania, 34–35, 39–40
    in Uganda, 22, 24, 26
Exports
    Kenya, 12, 15
    Rwanda-Burundi, 49, 51
    Tanzania, 40
    Uganda, 25

Freedom Struggle Association, 10.
    See also "Mau Mau"

Game reserves
    Kenya, 15
    Tanzania, 40
    See also Parks
Gautama, Khrishna, 11
German colonists
    in Rwanda-Urundi, 47
    in Tanzania, 34, 36
Giraffe, photo of, 14

Great Britain
    in Central Africa, 47
    in Uganda, 24
    See also British East Africa
        Company
Great Rift Valley, 1, 54
Gubu, 29

Habarimano, General Juvenal, 48
Harambee, 11, 16
Health care
    Tanzania, 40, 42
    Uganda, 31
Hippopotamus, photo of, 53
Hospital, Tanzania, 41
Hutu, 45, 47–48, 54

Imana, 52
Imports
    Kenya, 15
    Rwanda-Burundi, 51
    Tanzania, 40
Indian Ocean, 5, 7, 12, 33
Industry
    Kenya, 15
    Rwanda-Burundi, 51
    Tanzania, 40
    Uganda, 25, 29
Interracial cooperation, 10–11
Islam
    in Rwanda-Burundi, 52
    in Tanzania, 39
    in Uganda, 22
    See also Religions

Jinja, 29
Johnstone. *See* Kenyata, Mzee Jomo

Kabaka palace, 27
Kagera National Park, 54

[58]

Religions
    Kenya, 16
    Rwanda-Burundi, 51–52
    Tanzania, 39–40
    Uganda, 22
Rwanda, 1–2, 21, 33, 45–53
Rwanda-Urundi, 45, 47, 48. *See also*
    Rwanda; Burundi

Sahel, 29
Saudi Arabia, 28
Savannas, 5
Secondary school, Nairobi, 17
Serengeti Reserve, 40
Slave trade in Tanzania and Zanzibar, 34
Snakes, native to East Central Africa, 5
Socialism, in Tanzania, 37–39
Somalia, 7
Stanley, Henry, 2
Starvation
    in other African countries, 29
    in Uganda, 29–30
Sudan, 7, 21
Swahili, 22, 34

Tanganyika, 36. *See also* Tanzania
Tanganyika African National Union
    (TANU), 36–37
Tanzania, 1–2, 5, 21, 28, 33–43, 49
Thuku, Henry, 9
Traditions of Kenya, 16, 19
Tourism
    importance to Kenya, 15
    reasons for, 2
    in Tanzania, 40

Trees native to East Central Africa, 4
Tutsi, 45–48, 52, 54
Twa, 45
Twin Kingdoms, The, 47–48, 52, 54. *See
    also* Rwanda; Burundi

Uganda, 1–2, 21–31
    geography of, 27–28, 33
    regions of, 26–27
Uhuru, 11, 25
Ukamba, 18
Urundi. *See* Burundi. *See also* Rwanda-
    Urundi.

"White Highlands, The," 9
Wildlife
    importance to Kenya, 15
    in Rwanda-Burundi, 54
    in Tanzania, 40
    types native to East Central Africa,
    1–2
World War I
    effect on Rwanda-Burundi, 47
    effect on Tanzania, 36
    effect on Uganda, 25
World War II
    effect on Tanzania, 36
    effect on Uganda, 25

Zaire, 21, 33, 49
Zambia, 33
Zanzibar, 34–37
Zimbabwe, 29

[60]